TRACK
CHRISTIAN
LIFE

ABIGAIL
DODDS
SERIES EDITED BY
JOHN PERRITT

A STUDENT'S GUIDE TO
WOMANHOOD

CHRISTIAN
FOCUS

Copyright © Abigail Dodds 2022

paperback ISBN 978-1-5271-0842-4

ebook ISBN 978-1-5271-0918-6

10 9 8 7 6 5 4 3 2 1

First published in 2022
by
Christian Focus Publications Ltd,
Geanies House, Fearn, Ross-shire,
IV20 1TW, Great Britain
www.christianfocus.com

with

Reformed Youth Ministries,
1445 Rio Road East
Suite 201D
Charlottesville,
Virginia, 22911

Cover by MOOSE77
Printed by Bell & Bain, Glasgow

CONTENTS

For Eliza, Elianna, and Evangeline

May you be daughters in the Son—
fearless in the face of frightening things,
laughing at what's to come,
with an inner beauty that's imperishable,
stretching out your hands to do good,
holy women,
because you hope in God.

Series Introduction

Christianity is a religion of words, because our God is a God of words. He created through words, calls Himself the Living Word, and wrote a book (filled with words) to communicate to His children. In light of this, pastors and parents should take great efforts to train the next generation to be readers. *Track* is a series designed to do exactly that.

Written for students, the *Track* series addresses a host of topics in three primary areas: Doctrine, Culture, and the Christian Life. *Track's* booklets are theologically rich, yet accessible. They seek to engage and challenge the student without dumbing things down.

One definition of a track reads: *a way that has been formed by someone else's footsteps.* The goal of the *Track* series is to point us to that 'someone else'—Jesus Christ. The One who forged a track to guide His followers. While we cannot follow this track perfectly, by His grace and Spirit He calls us to strive to stay on the path. It is our prayer that this series of books would help guide Christ's Church until He returns.

In His service,

John Perritt
RYM's Director of Resources
Series Editor

1. Introduction

Writing a 'guide to womanhood' seems so simple and ordinary as to be unnecessary, but also as complicated and extraordinary as to be almost impossible—which, we will see, is partly a sign of the times we live in. Our world is very confused about womanhood (and manhood) and it takes a fair amount of untangling to address something so snarled. But also, being a woman is simultaneously simple and complex by God's design—it is glorious and mundane; it is particular and broad. It is a reality that exists apart from our willingness to consent to it, but one that also inhabits our very selves. That is what it means to exist as a created thing—that your willingness to agree with how or what you've been made has no bearing on who or what you actually are. The sun is unbothered by my professing it to be the moon. It keeps on burning, providing light and warmth for all.

The moon isn't affected in the least by my futile attempts to label it a star.

So too with womanhood. It does not need our mental assent to continue being what it is. Womanhood exists. Period. God made it so. No amount of railing against it or wishing it away can change that. And, what I'd like all of us to see is that womanhood is not something that we want to wish away. It's not something to be railed against, but received with gratitude. It cannot withstand idolizing, nor should it be relegated to the status of inconsequential.

Womanhood matters the way the walls of the house matter. It matters the way the food on the table matters. It matters the way flowers in the garden matter. It matters because God wanted it to matter—He made it consequential. But we don't direct our praise to walls or food or flowers. We praise the *Maker* of those things. We praise the Builder, the Provider, and the Gardener, for from *Him* and through *Him* and to *Him* are all things (Rom. 11:36). He gets all the glory for His glorious creation of womanhood.

OUR RECENT HISTORY

The past 100 years have seen great societal changes for women—both in how women think of themselves and how others think of them. The

1960s brought about a second wave of feminism, which, while seeking the empowerment of women, did so by making manhood the standard for women. They thought that being a powerful woman was achieved by becoming just like powerful men. Feminists wanted to be equal and interchangeable with men, which perhaps unintentionally ended up devaluing the things that made them distinctly women. They wanted women to be free from the 'burdens' of marriage, motherhood, and family life—free to have sex without 'consequences' (that is, children), free to kill their own offspring in the womb—in short, their desired freedom actually led to a horrid enslavement to sin.

Furthermore, they did not imagine that one day men might want to be equal and interchangeable with women—and by that, I mean the transgender movement. There are biological men who call themselves women, who are now allowed into women's restrooms, and even set records in women's sporting events. The trans movement makes a mockery of the female body, renaming breastfeeding, 'chest-feeding,' and women, 'birthing people.' And there are also biological women who call themselves men—who also take hormones to feel more masculine and, in some cases, mutilate their body to make it look like a man's body.

These changes are remarkable when you step back and look at the scope of human history. For the entire course of mankind, everyone knew who was a woman and who was a man. It was determined by the body God gave you. But in this unique moment in time, this moment God appointed you to live in, the loudest and most powerful voices in our society say that being a man or a woman has nothing to do with your body, but only your feelings. This is a serious lie with grave consequences. Yet even so, we know that sin is not new. It is as old as the garden of Eden. Yet it manifests in seemingly new ways, like a new cancer or virus. Sin is finding more and more outrageous ways to deceive and harm.

WHO AM I?

This basic question lies at the heart of so much human striving—it reveals a quest for self-knowledge. Many find it difficult to answer, as though the self is a mystery beyond finding out. I would like to suggest to you that answering the question, 'Who am I?' is actually not difficult, because the answer is given to us by assignment, not by self-reflection. Who am I? I am Abigail, a woman, a Christian, a daughter, a mother, a friend, a wife, a created person. All those fundamental things are not something I discovered about myself by taking an in-depth personality test. They are fundamentally gifts from a good Giver.

This is not a book to help you discover who you are, because who you are is a gift given to you by God that simply is, but rather, this is a book to help you receive with gladness who you are and to understand the meaning and purpose of who you are, namely, a woman made by God and saved through Christ.

I won't trifle with you or speak condescendingly to you in these pages. I'm assuming you want to think deeply. I'm assuming you don't want to be coddled like a child, but rather afforded the dignity of being told the straight truth and loved with the unsentimental pure love of Christ. This book is not a safe space as our culture defines it, because the truth of God's Word isn't the kind of safe that keeps us comfortable or secure in this world. Rather, it is the kind of safe that makes us secure in another world. Let's set our hope there—in heaven—where Christ is seated at God's right hand, and in doing so, may we become fearless women who hope in God.

Main point

There are many confused views about womanhood, but we will only find a true understanding of our created being by looking to our Creator.

Questions for Reflection

- What is a woman? Can you define 'woman' in a way that accords with God's Word?
- What are some things you've been taught about womanhood? Do these things match up with what the Bible teaches? If you don't know, how can you find out?
- Have you ever thought of womanhood as a gift to be received from God? How would thinking about it that way change your perception of being a woman?

2. From Chaos to Creation and Back Again

In the beginning, God created the heavens and the earth. The earth was without form and void, and darkness was over the face of the deep. And the Spirit of God was hovering over the face of the waters. And God said, 'Let there be...' (Gen. 1:1-3)

'Try saying towel,' I told my kids as we barreled down the freeway toward home. They were on a quest to discover which words would deconstruct as you said them over and over again. Have you ever tried it? It's as though the word disintegrates in your mouth, becoming only utterances of consonants and vowels. The parts replace the sum; mere letters replace the word. Nonsense replaces meaning.

I was reminded of C. S. Lewis's commentary on self-consciousness:

...it is disastrous when instead of merely attending to a rose we are forced to think of ourselves looking at the rose, with a certain type of mind and certain type of eyes. It is disastrous because, if you are not very careful, the colour of the rose gets attributed to our optic nerves and its scent to our noses, and in the end there is no rose left.

'NO ROSE LEFT'

Lewis's description is similar to the phenomenon my kids were searching for in the car—that is to say, there is a kind of attentiveness, a kind of seeing or saying or tasting or touching or hearing, that ultimately deconstructs the thing to which its attention is fixed. A word is no longer a word. A rose is no longer a rose. A man is no longer a man. A woman is no longer a woman. When our perceptions overtake the thing they are perceiving, they become a reality bigger than the thing itself, leaving the thing itself behind.

A spoken word becomes no more than the noise that hits my eardrums, a rose no more than the scent in my nose and the glint in my eye, a man no more than muscle fibers and cells and hair and appendages; so, too, with a woman. Therefore, who is to say that certain curves or types of appendages or amount of muscle fibers could in any way distinguish between male and female? And perhaps even more to the point, who would dare to assign meaning to such a collection of parts? Lewis instructs us again in *The Voyage of the Dawn Treader*, '"In our world", said Eustace, "a star is a huge ball of flaming gas". "Even in your world, my son, that is not what a star is, but only what it is made of."'

RE-CREATING CHAOS

Before God created the world, 'the earth was without form and void, and darkness was over the face of the deep. And the Spirit of God was hovering over the face of the waters' (Gen. 1:2). Into this dark chaos—this formless disorder—God's voice spoke order, meaning, light! Raw materials were shaped and fashioned with purpose and meaning. Was there ever such a perfectly productive word as the Word of the Lord? With His great wisdom, all He spoke came to pass.

Yet, we know how the story goes. Evil lurked in the shadows, waiting for its opportunity to corrupt the 'very good' pinnacle of God's work: mankind. When the cunning serpent spoke to

Eve, his words were not perfectly productive, they were perfectly destructive. And she succumbed to his temptation. Swallowing Satan's lies whole, she spat out the good words of instruction from her Creator. Mistrust was her food, cynicism her lens, and pride her destination. Adam's fall began the slow unraveling—the slow de-creation toward chaos and death from the order and life God had spoken.

And lo, these millennia later, in the twenty-first century, we are experiencing the sharp pain of that descent into chaos even still—perhaps never quite as acutely as in the upheaval around manhood and womanhood. Men and women have been reduced to one's own sense of things, just as with my repetition of the word 'towel' or Lewis's rose. The unrelenting attentions to sex and gender have only served to deconstruct them and make them nonsensical. America has no monuments to Baal or goddess temples to show for our spiritual pride; rather our own feelings are the new Baal: human perception is the new goddess that demands a sacrifice. And the sacrifices we have offered in worship to our human selves have been great indeed.

SCOTCH TAPE HUMANITY

Into the western world's self-wrought chaos and confusion over what we are, many are trying with all their might to speak loudly enough to drown out the ever-present voice of the Lord that continues to create day after day after day. God continues to cause the sun to rise, the rain to fall, and baby boys and girls to be knitted together in mothers' wombs. He continues to speak order into every cell and molecule—continues to weave meaning and purpose and design into existence. He continues to give to all: life and breath and everything (Acts 17:25).

But the voices of proud men and women shout rebellion, advocating for a humanity in which parts can be cut off, new ones attached, hormones administered, and renaming applied. The confusion over 'what we are' is not primarily a confusion about where we fall in the LGBT+ alphabet or so-called cis-gender identity. The confusion is over whether or not we are *God*. It's over whether we decide for ourselves what we are, or whether God decided what we would be before the foundation of the world. And it is from this fundamental seed of pride that all the other confusions grow.

As humanity de-creates itself, it then attempts to stand over the void of formlessness and chaos to speak its own words of self-making. Where there once was male, it speaks female. Where there once was girl, it speaks boy. Where there once was femininity, it speaks masculinity. Where there once was a design of fruitfulness, it speaks sterility. Our sinful, depraved, and poverty-stricken state means that even in our attempt to destroy the Maker's work, we must rely on that same God-supplied creation as the materials available to us to undo it and tape it back together upside down. We have no other material to work with.

And, just as God not only speaks reality into existence, He also declares truths about Himself in His speech (Ps. 19:1-6), so too in humanity's attempt to re-speak itself into something self-made, it reveals much about itself. The great revelation of sinful humanity is that, in our attempts to be God, in our great desire to speak forth something of meaning and substance apart from Him, we only ever speak the seeds of destruction. But there is Another who is like us, yet not like us, who offers us a newly-spoken word of life.

Main Point

Reducing 'male' and 'female' to constructed concepts that are interchangeable is a way of trying to be God.

Questions for Reflection

- Have your 'feelings' become idolatrous for you? Do you think 'feelings' have become idolatrous for your generation? If so, how?
- How might you take your feelings off the throne of your life and surrender to the Lord?
- Who gets to say what you are—you or God?

3. A Woman Reborn

In the beginning was the Word, and the Word was with God, and the Word was God. He was in the beginning with God. All things were made through him, and without him was not any thing made that was made. In him was life, and the life was the light of men. The light shines in the darkness, and the darkness has not overcome it. (John 1:1-5)

Our re-created chaos and darkness has met with Life and Light in the God-Man, Jesus. What's more, the Life found in the God-Man Jesus was see-able, touch-able, hear-able—in a word, it was perceivable to the senses. John testifies, 'That which was from the beginning, which we have heard, which we have seen with our eyes, which we looked upon and have touched with our hands, concerning the word of life—the life was made manifest, and we have seen it, and testify to it and proclaim to you the eternal life, which was with the Father and was made manifest to us' (1 John 1:1-2).

In Jesus, our senses, our perceptions—if we will get them on their knees before Him through the miraculous work of the Holy Spirit—will not deconstruct into madness and idolatry, but will bear witness to the greatest reality in the universe, namely, that God's Son is the Word by which all things were made, the Word by which all men and women must be saved, and the Word which recreates a new humanity that is being transformed into His likeness, from one degree of glory to the next.

The old humanity fell in Adam, the new humanity is buried and raised to life with Christ. The old humanity speaks destruction and death over itself and others, the new humanity speaks order and life as ambassadors of Jesus to all who would receive Him. The old humanity deconstructs through self-exaltation, the new humanity loses itself to gain Christ and, with Him, everything.

RE-ESTABLISHING WOMEN

If you are in Christ, then being born a woman is stuffed full of meaning and purpose and design. It's not that the meaning isn't there for non-Christians, it's that they cannot see it as they ought, because they rely only on their old eyes to apprehend it, not the new eyes and perceptions of those who trust Jesus. We have good news to share with them—we have hope for a redeemed humanity. We can call them to repentance and faith, to forgiveness of sins through the Lord's atoning death and to fullness of life as women.

In Christ, being a woman is a sturdy and stable reality to which objectively good meaning and purpose belong. In Christ, motherhood is both a physical and spiritual reality, in which the two do not compete, but complement one anoter. In Christ, the physical work of keeping and managing a home connects not only to doing good in this life, but stretches into the life to come, as it points forward to our eternal home in God. In Christ, a woman's submission to her own husband isn't an arbitrary assignment, but a fitting way to reflect the gospel as the weaker vessel. In Christ, being a sister means being a co-laborer and a true member of God's family. In Christ, being a daughter means having an inheritance from our Father—it is a forever reality that has already begun.

Do you balk at some of these descriptions? Maybe you've heard fierce debates over women's God-given roles, and even around the word 'submission.' We'll get into this later. For now, the simple truth is this: the world is in desperate need of Christian boys and girls, Christian sons and daughters, Christian brothers and sisters, Christian fathers and mothers, Christian uncles and aunts, Christian grandfathers and grandmothers. At a time when the rejection of one's created self is posing as the ultimate self-love, when the mutilation of the body is being sold as kindness, Christians must be bold in affirming the goodness of male and female and beckoning the wayward sons and daughters home to their Heavenly Father.

Our womanhood was spoken by God through Christ in the beginning. And for women who have been born again—re-created by Jesus, the Word made flesh—our womanhood has been redeemed from the curse of sin. Our new life in Him is not gender neutral, rather our bodies and DNA exist through Him and for Him. So now, we offer our bodies, our female bodies, as living sacrifices to Him, putting every bit of our trust in the unbreakable statute of His Word.

Main Point

*Being a woman in Christ is full of meaning,
purpose, and design.*

Questions for Reflection

- How do you think most unbelievers view manhood and womanhood? Why?
- Does being a Christian change the way you view being a woman? How and why?
- Reflect on the fact that God designed a world where both man and woman, father and mother, grandmother and grandfather, aunt and uncle, son and daughter, sister and brother were good and necessary. What does that communicate about Him?

4. Commissioned With Our Bodies

Therefore a man shall leave his father and his mother and hold fast to his wife, and they shall become one flesh. And the man and his wife were both naked and were not ashamed. (Gen. 2:24-25)

In third grade, our gym teacher made us run a mile. It was part of a physical fitness assessment that they did every year, but our first exposure to it was in third grade. We were marched out to the grass surrounding the tennis courts and told to run around them so many times. I wish I could remember the exact number of times, but I know however many times it was seemed ridiculous and impossible to my third-grade self. Even so, as the teacher described what we were to do, I could feel my competitive juices begin to flow—surges of adrenaline made my heart pound as she showed us the starting line. My dad was a runner, so the little I knew of competitive running came from tips I'd heard and observed from him. Don't start out too fast. Keep an even pace. Save enough energy so that you can sprint to finish.

Our teacher was clear that this wasn't a race, but she couldn't fool us. Most of the students in the class were edging toward the front of the starting line, jostling for the best position. There were a few girls who seemed utterly unconcerned about the whole ordeal and were happily clustered together at the back. But most of us, boys and girls alike, were getting ready to prove ourselves.

A KIND OF WINNING THAT WOULDN'T LAST

I finished first that day by sheer will and determination. I couldn't have been prouder of myself, even as I resisted the urge to puke in the grass. Beating the boys in my class had a special euphoria to it, although not because I had been taught that I was less than boys and needed to show myself better. And not because I was lacking in love or affirmation from my parents or other adults in my life. I was cherished by both mother and father. I had healthy friendships with girls and boys. There were no awards or trophies for this 'win,' no tangible glory to be had, yet there was a different kind of glory I was after. It wasn't a pure desire to do my best and honor the Lord, it was a sick desire to get glory for myself in a way that made 'the boys' lesser, smaller, and most especially, beaten by a girl.

But that kind of glory would not be available to me for long. It didn't take too many years before the physical differences between me and the boys in my grade were substantial. They were taller, had more muscle, and, no matter how hard I gutted it out with sheer will and determination, I could not come in first when we ran the mile each subsequent year in gym class. I could always beat a number of them, but, when my best effort was put up against the best effort of a boy of similar fitness to me, I could not will myself to win. The body that belonged to him was able to finish the mile more quickly than the body that belonged to me.

You probably know that this reality—the reality that male bodies generally have more muscle mass and are larger than female bodies—is a reality that is being and has been obscured by almost everything we see in movies and media. It is ignored not only by feminists, but by the culture at large. It is downplayed in schools and classrooms. And if that weren't enough, the reverse is also true. Now, with the gender revolution, we have boys pretending their bodies can do things only female bodies can do, such as have periods or get pregnant. Once-trusted institutions such as the United States government are playing make-believe right along with them, using phrases like 'pregnant people' rather than pregnant women, and 'chest-feeding' rather than breastfeeding. This too is a kind of 'winning' that cannot last.

THE FIRST COMMISSION

In the earliest chapters of Genesis, God's words spoken into the cosmos bring forth all that is now created. Among the creation is humanity, made in His own image, male and female. He commissions them like this:

And God blessed them. And God said to them, 'Be fruitful and multiply and fill the earth and subdue it, and have dominion over the fish of the sea and over the birds of the heavens and over every living thing that moves on the earth.' And God said, 'Behold, I have given you every plant yielding seed that is on the face of all the earth, and every tree with seed in its fruit. You shall have them for food. And to every beast of the earth and to every bird of the heavens and to everything that creeps on the earth, everything that has the breath of life, I have given every green plant for food.' And it was so. And God saw everything that he had made, and behold, it was very good. (Gen. 1:28-31)

What is so obvious as to almost be forgotten is that both the male and female body were essential *to the mission.* There would be no 'fruitfulness' and no 'filling' and no 'subduing' and no 'dominion' without male bodies and female bodies that perfectly fit and complemented one another. The sexual union of one man and one woman in marriage is the prerequisite of obedience to God's mission for humanity as told to us in the first and second chapters of Genesis. Marriage is the norm—meaning that, from the beginning God intended for men and women to be married.

And the rib that the LORD God had taken from the man he made into a woman and brought her to the man. Then the man said,

'This at last is bone of my bones

and flesh of my flesh;
she shall be called Woman,
because she was taken out of Man.'

Therefore a man shall leave his father and his mother and hold fast to his wife, and they shall become one flesh. And the man and his wife were both naked and were not ashamed. (Gen. 2:22-25)

Our bodies testify to that pre-fall reality, if imperfectly. Female bodies are equipped with female parts: wombs, breasts, ovaries, and eggs. Our bodies fit together with the male body in such a way that both bodies are doing what they were designed to do. The man's body gives seed, the woman's body grows life—all in the context of a loving union for life. The man's body is well-suited to guard and defend; the woman's body is well-suited to nurture and sustain. God calls this design 'very good.' He came up with it. He desires to fill the world with people made in His own image. He wants His world full to the brim with His glory—and godly offspring are part of the display of His glory.

Prior to sin entering the world, there would have been no marring to this design—no compartmentalizing the body away from the life of the mind. No separation between body and soul that would make one spiritual and the other earthly. No dysfunction of any kind—not in the body's abilities or the emotional relationship between the husband and wife. Of course, sin has made this commission much more difficult, even impossible in some sense. But, even so, it's good for us to acquaint ourselves with the mission God gave Adam and Eve—to remind ourselves of what God is after. He wants the world full of people who reflect Him and display His glory.

When God gave this first commission to Adam and Eve, He was giving them a blessing. But, the curse of sin followed closely and, thankfully, so did the promise of a new covenant with a new commission.

Main point

Physical differences between men and women are real, and they are part of God's original good plan for the world.

Questions for Reflection

- What do you think it means to be made in God's image?

- Have you ever seriously thought about the commission given to Adam and Eve in Genesis? What do you think it means for us today?
- How are men's and women's physical bodies integral for God's mission? Does this fact cause any reaction from you?

5. Recommissioned for Righteousness

Let not sin therefore reign in your mortal body, to make you obey its passions. Do not present your members to sin as instruments for unrighteousness, but present yourselves to God as those who have been brought from death to life, and your members to God as instruments for righteousness. (Rom. 6:12-13)

When it comes to the design for male and female seen in our bodies and outlined in Genesis and other parts of Scripture, I find that there are often three responses to this God-given design: rebellion, resentment, and good resolve. The rebellious response is the one driving my third-grade desire to 'beat the boys' at all costs. But the more grown-up forms of rebellion are as present in self-pity (an inseparable cousin to resentment) as they are in pride.

Rebelling against the female body God has given you may look extreme, like gender reassignment surgeries or embracing gender fluidity or other forms of self-harm, such as cutting or drugs. Rebellion can also mean idolizing our female body (or getting others to idolize it), over-primping and preening so as to use it for power and control through sexting or promiscuity. In these rebellious acts, we take up our womanhood (and our female bodies) as a weapon to wield against others, rather than a purposeful gift from God to be received.

Others respond to God's gift of womanhood with resentment because they feel He has not delivered on His part of the bargain. If marriage is the design for humanity, then why are so many women still single? If fruitfulness is part of the mission, then why do some face infertility? If dominion is our calling, then why am I struggling with this physical disability? If all these things are part of His design, then why is He keeping them from me? These painful questions arise from those who desperately *want* to fulfill the Genesis commission, not from those who are actively rebelling against it. Yet, blaming God or becoming suspicious toward Him because of what He hasn't given is dangerous ground to tread, even as we may mourn and lament what we don't have.

Lastly, we can respond to God's design with good resolve. I've observed women who refuse to belittle God's call on their lives as women, despite the most difficult circumstances that would tempt them to forsake it. These women resolve to agree with what God says, no matter how foolish the world thinks they are. Good resolve is not blindness to difficulties. It is not a happy-go-lucky attitude or the wearing of rose-colored glasses. Living with good resolve to receive God's design for womanhood, despite difficulties and trials, is simply an outworking of living by faith in God's Son—that means that in all circumstances, even the circumstance of our being born a woman, we entrust ourselves by faith in Jesus to our Sovereign God.

A NEW COMMISSION FOR A GROANING WORLD

The story of Eve's encounter with the serpent in Genesis 3 gives us understanding of the curse of sin and its thwarting power in regard to fulfilling our call to be fruitful and multiply. And so it is that our bodies are now exposed to the groaning effects of sin on all creation, meaning infertility, disability, and disease. 'For the creation was subjected to futility, not willingly, but because of him who subjected it, in hope that the creation itself will be set free from its bondage to corruption and obtain the freedom of the glory of the children of God.' (Rom. 8:20-21)

From the earliest stories of God's people—even with Abraham's own wife and granddaughter-in-law—we see how unwanted barrenness can grow into hardened resentment when it is not brought before the Lord in prayer and vulnerability. Hannah's prayers and tears for a child are the template for a woman who acts righteously in her tears and sorrow and heartache. Yet, the new covenant reminds us of *eternal* fruitfulness—fruitfulness that is not dependent on a body that can have babies. It tells us of a fruitfulness that will mark every single believer.

In other words, the curse of sin is death, so mere physical fruitfulness cannot fulfill the Genesis commission as it ought to have done, because that fruitfulness will not last— everyone will die. Rather, *lasting life*, lasting fruitfulness comes in our being reborn through Christ who crushed death and the curse of sin by His perfect life, death, and resurrection. This does not make the Genesis commission obsolete, but it does make it incomplete. We still need men and women to marry and have children. But more than that, we need their children to be *born again* through faith in Jesus Christ. And we need both the married and unmarried alike to participate in the Great Commission given by Jesus: 'Go therefore and make disciples of all nations, baptizing them in the name of the Father and of the Son and of the Holy Spirit, teaching them to observe all that I have commanded you. And behold, I am with you always, to the end of the age' (Matt. 28:19-20).

In this new commission, every Christian woman is fruitful through the making of disciples—be they her biological children or the kids in her Sunday school class or the troubled youth of our neighborhoods or the nations. We are all called to pour forth the fruit of the Spirit in our daily lives, doing the work of spiritual mothers, welcoming as many as will come to the marriage supper of the Lamb at the end of the age when all things will be made new. Our spiritual sons and daughters are made righteous through trust in Christ.

EVERY MEMBER AN INSTRUMENT OF RIGHTEOUSNESS

In Paul's letter to the Romans, he hits on this topic of our physical bodies, probably most famously in Romans 12, 'I appeal to you therefore, brothers, by the mercies of God, to present your bodies as a living sacrifice, holy and acceptable to God, which is your spiritual worship.' (Rom. 12:1)

Since I was young, I have loved this verse. The part that always clung to me was the phrase, 'living sacrifice.' It helped me reorient everything I did during the day to think of myself as a sacrifice to God, a sacrifice that was alive! It wasn't until much later that the phrase, 'present your bodies' began to make me think more deeply about what Paul meant with his appeal. What did my physical body have to do with my spiritual life?

Earlier in his letter to the Romans, Paul makes plain the importance of our physical bodies in relation to our spiritual life. He says this:

Let not sin therefore reign in your mortal body, to make you obey its passions. Do not present your members to sin as instruments for unrighteousness, but present yourselves to God as those who have been brought from death to life, and your members to God as instruments for righteousness. For sin will have no dominion over you, since you are not under law but under grace. (Rom. 6:12-14)

Here in Romans 6 is the inverse of what Paul says in Romans 12:1. Rather than tell us to 'present our bodies,' he tells us 'do not present your members' ('members' is a word for the parts of your body). Our bodies are to be instruments of righteousness, not slaves of sin. John Calvin says, 'The goal of God's work in us is to bring our lives into harmony and agreement with His own righteousness,'—this righteousness is more than mental agreement, but agreement in the very members of our body as we walk in a way that pleases Him.

By the fruit of the Spirit called self-control, we are empowered by that Spirit to first take dominion over our own bodies, telling our hands, 'Stretch out to that person in need,' and our eyes, 'Stop looking at that image,' and our legs, 'Keep trudging up the hill until that job is done.' And as women, we have different bodies to present to God for righteousness than the men do. We have many things in common, but also several things that are distinct. And know this—whatever sins you've committed with your body can be forgiven by the blood of Jesus. There is nothing your body has done or experienced that can keep you from coming to God in repentance and faith. He receives you because of His great love for you that caused Him to send His Son to offer His body as a sacrifice for our sins. His body was crushed for our iniquities, our impurities, our sinfulness, so that whatever sins we've committed can now be forgiven and cleansed. And what's more, Christ's body is now raised to life so that we too can hope to have our bodies resurrected and made new and whole again some day.

What a joy to offer to God all of ourselves—to give to Him our whole hearts, our whole bodies, our whole selves—for we have died with Christ and have been raised with Him, so that nothing offered to Him by faith in Christ is ever lost. Our resurrected bodies in the new heavens and new earth will be fully and finally consecrated to Him, unable to sin, and glorified forever.

Main point

We live in a broken world where our bodies are not perfect, but God calls us to live for Him, whatever the circumstances.

Questions for Reflection

- Have you found yourself responding in rebellion or resentment when it comes to the design of your physical body? How can you move toward responding with good resolve?
- In what way is the Genesis commission still needed—and in what way is it incomplete?
- How might your life change if you offered yourself, your whole body, as a living sacrifice to God every day?

6. Whole-Hearted Women Shaped by the Whole Council of God

For the word of God is living and active, sharper than any two-edged sword, piercing to the division of soul and of spirit, of joints and of marrow, and discerning the thoughts and intentions of the heart. And no creature is hidden from his sight, but all are naked and exposed to the eyes of him to whom we must give account. (Heb. 4:12-13)

The first book of the Bible I remember reading straight through was the book of James. I was about eleven or twelve years old and, up to that point, my Bible reading had been like popcorn prayers: rather than short prayers, I read short passages—bite-sized bits here and there accompanied by somebody else's insights in the form of a devotional. But this read-through of James was different from my previous encounters with the Bible. I couldn't stop reading. I didn't want to stop reading.

Every word held me captive, holding up a mirror to my face, piercing my heart, and illuminating my path.

Over time, I read more and more of God's Word, and I found that what was true of the book of James was true of other books of the Bible, too. I was held captive by God's voice. That's not to say I found every book of the Bible easy to understand. I certainly didn't. There were parts that puzzled me completely. But, even in the parts that were difficult for me to grasp, or in the places where I felt a bit lost in the history of God's people or laws or genealogies, I still could recognize God's penetrating voice.

As I got into my teenage years, I ditched the devotionals and began simply reading book by book by book. Now, at age forty, I've read the Bible through over and over and over again. I've soaked in its hard-to-understand passages. I've reveled in its gloriously simple passages. I've heard and re-heard and heard afresh the voice of God in the pages of His book. And can I tell you something? Nothing has been as transformative for my life. Nothing has provided me the nourishment for my soul that the Scriptures have provided. Nothing has corrected me, rebuked me, encouraged me, strengthened me, upheld me, reminded me, kept me, taught me, trained me, and equipped me like God has with His own words written down for us in the Bible. Nothing has made me into a Christian woman like God's powerful Word has. I'm proof that His Word does not return void. And so are you, if you have been made alive by the Word of His power through faith in Jesus Christ.

NO PICKY EATERS

You see, God's words are meant to be consumed, every day, like food. In order to stay alive, we must eat His Word. A Christian woman who is on a starvation diet when it comes to God's Word is in danger of not being a Christian woman at all. The prophet Jeremiah says this,

Your words were found, and I ate them,
and your words became to me a joy
and the delight of my heart,
for I am called by your name,
O LORD, God of hosts. (Jer. 15:16)

And David proclaims, 'Oh, taste and see that the LORD is good! Blessed is the man who takes refuge in him!' (Ps. 34:8) This means that from Genesis to Revelation, God is telling us about

49

Himself. He's telling us what He loves and what He hates. He's telling us what kind of God He is—showing us what holiness is like, what justice is like, what love is like, what wrath is like, what mercy is like—He shows us what these things are as He shows us Himself, because those things don't exist apart from Him. We don't get to decide on our own definition of love, then apply it to God. We don't come up with a plan for justice, then check to see if God is following our plan. Instead, we start with God. We let Him define those realities for us in the Scriptures. And we, by faith, submit ourselves to Him, no matter what.

It can be tempting to ignore parts of the Bible, to only read or think about the things that give us a little uplifting feeling each day. But this is not the way we know God. We would not like it very much if a dear friend decided that she only wanted to speak with us on Wednesday mornings. And that our love of hiking was an embarrassment to her, so she pretended we actually loved knitting instead. To top it off, she thought our name was a little outdated, so she had taken to calling us by a new name that was nothing like our real name. That would be an unhealthy and manipulative friendship indeed. Yet many people treat God that way—as their plaything, their possession. The difference is that God is never mocked and He will have the final word.

WHOLE HEARTS OBEY GOD

When God saved you from sin and death by making you alive through faith in His Son, He fulfilled a prophecy spoken by the prophet Jeremiah. 'And I will give you a new heart, and a new spirit I will put within you. And I will remove the heart of stone from your flesh and give you a heart of flesh. And I will put my Spirit within you, and cause you to walk in my statutes and be careful to obey my rules.' (Ezek. 36:26–27)

Christian women have new hearts. Whole hearts. Hearts that incline toward God and His Word, not away from it. This doesn't mean that we never go through dry seasons, or that Bible reading is always easy for us or that every bit of reading we do is a ten on the scale of 'life-changing.' Rather, Christian women have hearts where God's Spirit resides and His Spirit is helping us to be tender toward Him—alive, soft, beating. The Christian woman's heart loves God and wants to keep His commands, not as a way of earning salvation, but because she has been saved and His ways are good and true and beautiful to her. So what should we do if our hearts feel old, hard, and disinclined toward God?

There are three ways to help our hearts remember to whom they belong. The first is to pray. Ask God to make your heart alive to Him! Ask Him for the miracle of a new, whole heart! Ask Him to reawaken your heart to Him if it has grown cold.

Second, repent of any sin in your life that you've been ignoring or willfully doing. Have you been lying to your parents? Tell God; tell them. Turn to the truth. Have you been looking at porn? Tell God; tell a believer. Turn to sexual purity with your eyes. Have you been addicted to social media and what people think of you? Tell God; tell a believer. Turn away from worthless things and live to please God alone. Sin makes us numb to God. It deadens our hearts. It hardens our consciences. It silences our prayers. It keeps us from the good that God has for us in His Word. It ruins our lives. But confessed, repented of, sin cannot keep us from God. It has no more power. So don't delay—go to Him, right now, receive His forgiveness and walk in newness of life.

Third, read God's Word, even if you don't feel like it. We cannot be alive to God if we don't know who He is. We cannot love Him or obey Him if we don't know Him or what He commands. We cannot receive the Good News of the Gospel—that Jesus came to earth as a man, lived, died, and was resurrected to save sinners—if we aren't reminding ourselves of it day by day.

The Apostle John says that this whole world is in the power of the evil one (1 John 5:19). This means that, for the world, sinning is normal. Sinning is the air the world breathes. And the evil one wants you to think that sinning is normal—that it is no big deal. Because when we succumb to that—when we start to feel 'normal' in our sin, that's when righteousness, goodness, and holiness begin to seem strange, weird, unattractive, far away, and even foolish. But you, dear sister, have been washed of your sin, cleansed of your iniquity, and given a new heart. God's Spirit lives in you. Because of Christ, righteousness is your new normal— that's what it means to be a Christian woman.

Main Point

God's Word transforms us and enables us to see the world through His eyes.

Questions for Reflection

- Do you desire to read God's Word, or has your appetite dried up? Take a minute to pray for God to awaken your appetite for His Word and to help you be disciplined in your reading of it.
- Are there parts of God's Word that you avoid reading because they're confusing or distasteful to you? Are there parts that you return to frequently?
- With whom can you partner as you read all of God's Word? Is there a family member or friend who would get on the same Bible reading plan with you so that you could check-in with one another and occasionally discuss what you're reading?

7. Womanly Virtues and Virtuous Women

'Many women have done excellently,
   but you surpass them all.'
Charm is deceitful, and beauty is vain,
   but a woman who fears the LORD is to be
praised.
Give her of the fruit of her hands,
   and let her works praise her in the gates.
(Prov. 31:29-31)

Social media has myriad faults and temptations, but one thing Instagram is good for (for me at least) is inspiration to try something new or get going on something old. The best accounts for me to follow are ones that are teaching something like gardening, cooking, knitting, home decorating, painting, or something fun and creative like that. 'Pasta Grannies' is the name of an account that documents old women in Italy who make pasta by hand. I'm not Italian and I have no particular love of pasta, but watching the weathered hands of grandmothers work to roll, cut, and shape pasta noodles made me wish I had such a heritage. Their speed, their precision, and the incredible muscle memory that makes the whole process second nature to them, makes it clear they've given a significant portion of their life to making food for others. There is love in it.

Often, what I glean from accounts like these is a reminder of the necessity of diligence and hard work, even more than the particular skill they're sharing with the world. And so, as long as I hop off Instagram and let that spark of inspiration help me dig into the work in front of me, then virtue has won.

DIRECT INSTRUCTIONS FOR YOU

The Bible is written to a broad audience. During ancient times, both men and women were present for the reading of the Torah. Much of the New Testament is written to the Christian church and would have been read aloud to gathered believers—men, women, and children. Within the Bible, we hear stories told of men and women—sometimes stories of godliness and virtue, sometimes stories of great sin and destruction. Most of the instructions we hear in the Bible are applied to men and women alike, but we also hear particular and distinct instructions for men and women.

Sometimes it's those particular instructions to us women that can rub us the wrong way because they are so different than what we are hearing in the world around us. Here's a brief sampling:

1. *I desire then that in every place the men should pray, lifting holy hands without anger or quarreling; likewise also that women should adorn themselves in respectable apparel, with modesty and self-control, not with braided hair and gold or pearls or costly attire, but with what is proper for women who profess godliness—with good works. Let a woman learn quietly with all submissiveness. I do not permit a woman to teach or to exercise authority over a man; rather, she is to remain quiet. For Adam was formed first, then Eve; and Adam was not deceived, but the woman was deceived and became a transgressor. Yet she will be saved through childbearing—if they continue in faith and love and holiness, with self-control. (1 Tim. 2:8-15)*

2. *But as for you, teach what accords with sound doctrine. Older men are to be sober-minded,*

dignified, self-controlled, sound in faith, in love, and in steadfastness. Older women likewise are to be reverent in behavior, not slanderers or slaves to much wine. They are to teach what is good, and so train the young women to love their husbands and children, to be self-controlled, pure, working at home, kind, and submissive to their own husbands, that the word of God may not be reviled. (Titus 2:1-5)

3. *Likewise, wives, be subject to your own husbands, so that even if some do not obey the word, they may be won without a word by the conduct of their wives, when they see your respectful and pure conduct. Do not let your adorning be external—the braiding of hair and the putting on of gold jewelry, or the clothing you wear—but let your adorning be the hidden person of the heart with the imperishable beauty of a gentle and quiet spirit, which in God's sight is very precious. For this is how the holy women who hoped in God used to adorn themselves, by submitting to their own husbands, as Sarah obeyed Abraham, calling him lord. And you are her children, if you do good and do not fear anything that is frightening. (1 Pet. 3:1-6)*

These passages (and others—think Proverbs 31) have caused no small amount of angst among women, at times offending and embittering them, at times confusing them, and at times becoming the sum total of their Christian life—replacing faith in Christ with womanly works' righteousness. What I desire for you to see is that God *does* emphasize certain things to women, but not as a replacement for the gospel, but rather as a glorious outworking of it. And I'd like to convince you that those things are worth paying attention to, worth thinking about and working at. But those things can't save you any more than any good work can save you. But they do testify to Christ at work in you, just as all good works do.

So, what virtues does God emphasize when it comes to women? Just from the passages above, we can find holiness, purity, fearlessness in the face of frightening things, self-control, reverence, truthful speech, moderation in regard to alcohol, kindness, modesty, inner beauty, gentleness, a quiet spirit, fear of the Lord, hard work, and—in the case of married women—submissiveness to their own husbands, and love of and care for their families. It's quite a list, and it's not even an exhaustive one of everything God specifically instructs women to be and do.

Why do you suppose God made sure that women were given specific instructions, especially when many—you could even argue *all*—of the virtues apply to men as well? I think it's because God made women and He knows the particular distinctions we have from men and that we need certain things highlighted. God thought it was important to remind us women that our outer beauty is not what we should be focusing on, but rather, our inner beauty is what matters to Him. He never says it quite like that to the men.

I don't think it's too much of a stretch to suppose that he never says it like that to the men because men aren't usually as pretty as women. Generally speaking, women are the fairer sex, which just means they are nicer to look at. And that's no small gift from God! But we mustn't abuse that gift: being nicer to look at means we will be getting more attention for how we look, which means we may be tempted to spend more time than is good for us trying to look a certain way. Or to value our outside appearance more than our character, and to compare ourselves to others. But, even if I'm wrong about *why* God tells women to be modest when it comes to their clothes and hair and jewelry, it doesn't change the fact that He, in His omniscience and sovereignty, does in fact tell us that. He knew we needed to hear it.

THE VIRTUOUS WOMEN IN THE PAGES AND THE PEWS

The direct instructions given to women by God are helpful, yet I'm thankful God has also given us examples. Remember the 'Pasta Grannies'? Even though they did not proclaim Christ, I, as a Christian, gleaned from their diligence and devotion to making good food for their families. The Proverbs 31 woman is the most famous example of a virtuous woman, even if she is a sort of figurative representation of the ideal—it is still worth aspiring to the godly traits she represents. And even as God gives us instructions in 1 Peter, He points us to a particular woman, Abraham's wife, Sarah, as the model of a holy woman who hoped in God by her submissiveness, good works, and fearlessness. It's interesting that so few people who talk about women in the Bible point to Sarah as an example for us, since she is the most explicit example of godliness we have in the Old Testament. I make this observation so that we won't similarly ignore Sarah. We have much to learn from her godliness. We want to be her daughters.

And there are so many more examples! We have Rahab and Ruth and Esther and the Hebrew midwives. These women put flesh on the direct instructions God has given us. They help us see it lived out. We may never be put in their shoes—we live in a different time and different circumstances. But, the principles of godliness are still there for us to glean from.

And they aren't the only ones who show us principles of godliness lived out; our sisters who sit down the pew from us do, too. The women at your church, in your town—the ones working in the nurseries and kitchens, in the offices and helping with Bible studies— they can show you what it looks like to be a virtuous woman of God. And they have the added advantage of being able to talk with you, to answer your questions, to ask some of their own, to know you and be known by you. This is the pattern that God has for us—to learn from older women as He instructs in Titus 2. And if you can't—if you don't know of an older Christian woman at your church who could help to teach and train you in godliness, then make use of older women through podcasts and books and other means of grace. Read Elisabeth Elliot and Corrie Ten Boom and Helen Roseveare and Amy Carmichael. Listen to seasoned women and hold off on spending all your time listening to peers.

Besides all the good examples in the Scriptures and in our own lives, there are also bad examples. The Bible doesn't shy away from showing us wicked women and we ought to learn from these examples as well. Jezebel and Potipher's wife, and the false prophetesses of Ezekiel's day who wickedly prophesied from their own hearts, and Herodias's daughter who demanded the head of John the Baptist on a platter, all show us examples of ungodly, unholy women. We must not neglect learning from them about who not to be and what not to do.

THE WISEST OF WOMEN

My most beloved example of a godly woman in the Scriptures is Abigail (since she's my namesake). Abigail was married to a foolish man (thankfully, I don't share this in common with her), and we aren't told how she came into such a marriage. But despite being joined to a foolish husband, she exudes discretion and wisdom, intervening in a situation that would have likely resulted in much bloodshed, and rescuing King David from acting sinfully through her bold, yet discreet, action.

Proverbs 14:1 says, 'The wisest of women builds her house, but folly with her own hands tears it down.' Do you want to be wise? Do you want to be the *wisest*? Then build up the house God's given you. Not just the building or apartment or dorm room or structure, but all the things the house represents—the people in it, the relationships, the bonds of love and good will, the laughter, the music, the joy, the truthfulness, and the faith inside it. Abigail builds her house by saving it from destruction, doing good to her foolish husband and the King, and leaving her husband to the Lord's judgment. Without the foreknowledge that God would later rescue her from the marriage and make her a wife to the King, she builds her house. Jesus' friend Mary, the one who sits at His feet while Martha complains she's been left with all the serving, is wisely building her house. She's got her mind set on things that will last forever—the things of the Lord.

It's so easy to tear things down—to tear down people with our words and tear down trust by spreading gossip and tear down friendships through rumors and offense-taking. We tear down the members of our own house because we haven't learned to tame our biting tongues. But there is a better way, a wiser way. And because God has made us His own daughters, with the help of the Holy Spirit we can not only build our house—the people and household we're a part of—but we can be built as a member of His house, the church. He builds us into wise women and we get to be part of His house, made of living stones, that will last forever.

Main Point

God offers us wisdom on how to be godly women through direct instructions in His Word and examples of godliness both in Scripture and our own lives.

Questions for Reflection

- Have you spent much time considering the passages of Scripture that are directed toward women? What is your response to them?
- Why do you think God gives instructions to women that emphasize particular virtues?

- What's one example of a godly woman in Scripture or in real life that you want to imitate? Are there any examples of ungodly women that you want to avoid?

8. Romantic Love or Lack Thereof

He brought me to the banqueting house,
  and his banner over me was love. (Song. 2:4)

She called me late at night. My husband and I were both reading in bed. She was relieved and tired. Upon hearing her words, I was relieved and exuberant. 'We went for a walk tonight and I gave him the ring back. I called the wedding off.' The invitations, ready to be sent, would not make it to the mailbox. The venues, the dresses, the vendors—all would be canceled. Money was lost. But that was nothing to the grief of ending the hope of something good, the hope of a marriage.

Yet, the relief was real because the red flags and problems were real. This dear friend of mine had been wooed by someone who seemed wonderful, at first. He was a good student, a hard worker; he called himself a Christian, was from an intact family, he had respectable friends, and seemed to value the same things my friend did. But over time, some disturbing patterns began to emerge that couldn't be ignored: his jealousy and controlling nature—he was bothered by her close friendships; his obsession with my friend that was something different than the consuming infatuation of young love; and finally, his outburst of anger that resulted in violence toward her.

By the time my friend told me about the violent outburst, she was already beginning to come to her senses and see the significant character problems in the man she'd agreed to marry. Her courage to call it off when it would have been so easy to ignore the red flags as flukes or isolated problems is a testament to God's Holy Spirit at work in her. It is not easy to put an engagement ring back into the hand of the man who put it on your finger in great expectation only months prior, but it's a lot easier than being married to a man who is a fraud—whose selfishness leads him to try to dominate you rather than love you.

IS IT BETTER TO BE SINGLE OR MARRIED?

One of the somewhat difficult passages in Scripture is Paul's writing to the Corinthians about being married and being single. It's not terribly difficult because it's hard to understand, rather it can be uncomfortable because it bumps up against the realities of marriage and singleness—and both of those realities are very personal, very close to our hearts and desires, and can be difficult (and both of them can be glorious!). Paul, who was single, says,

> *I wish that all were as I myself am. But each has his own gift from God, one of one kind and one of another. To the unmarried and the widows I say that it is good for them to remain single, as I am. But if they cannot exercise self-control, they should marry. For it is better to marry than to burn with passion. (1 Cor. 7:7–9)*

Then just a little later he says, 'Only let each person lead the life that the Lord has assigned to him, and to which God has called him. This is my rule in all the churches.' (1 Cor. 7:17) One thing that becomes clear is that whether it's better to be married or single depends on what God has called you to—in other words, it depends on whether you've been called to singleness or to marriage. Paul seems to understand that the calling to singleness is unusual and that most of his readers will find his encouragement to be 'as he is' too difficult.

We know that from the beginning, God intended for man and woman to marry and be fruitful. So, Paul knows that it will take much self-control to choose not to exercise that God-given design. But he also knows that the calling to singleness can be a very fruitful calling because of how it allows one to be single-minded in their devotion to the Lord. Husbands are rightly concerned how to please their wives and wives are rightly concerned how to please their husbands, but a man or woman called to singleness is free to please the Lord alone.

HOW DO I KNOW MY CALLING?

The simple truth is, we don't exactly get to choose whether or not we get married. You may want to get married, but you may face a shortage of age-appropriate, godly, and eligible Christian men. At age twenty, you may think singleness is right for you, but God may place someone in your path that changes that—and quickly. All I'm saying is, none of us can see the future. Trying to figure out if you're called to marriage or singleness as a young person can often lead to an unhelpful elevation of our own sense of how our life might unfold.

None of us knows what God will assign to us in the circumstances of life. Human expectations of how our lives will play out toy with the arrogance that James speaks about,

> *Come now, you who say, 'Today or tomorrow we will go into such and such a town and spend a year there and trade and make a profit'—yet you do not know what tomorrow will bring. What is your life? For you are a mist that appears for a little time and then vanishes. Instead you ought to say, 'If the Lord wills, we will live and do this or that.' As it is, you boast in your arrogance. All such boasting is evil. (James 4:13–16)*

But, what makes every season, whether single or married, valuable and meaningful and completely worthwhile is knowing that every circumstance of your life comes from God's loving and powerful hand. It's not a fluke or an accident or a punishment. It is His plan. One way to discover your calling *today* is to look at what situation you're in today. Are you single? Then today you are called to singleness. Are you married? Then today (and for as long as you both shall live), you are called to marriage. John Calvin said, 'Holiness is the goal of our calling.' This is true for both married and single alike.

You may be called to lifelong singleness as Paul was, and in that case, I would guess that you will have more than a mild inkling that singleness is your long-term calling. I would guess you have a strong and unshakeable sense of God setting you apart for singleness. If you don't have that sense, but rather the opposite strong desire to be married, then just as every Christian must, you must submit to the circumstances of life that God has assigned to you right now. And do so with gratitude. He is not depriving you—He is growing you into the likeness of His perfect Son. Not one detail of your life is outside of His sovereign plan, not one speck of it escapes His promise that He is working *all things*—both romantic love and the lack thereof—together for the good of those who love Him. (Rom. 8:28)

As you submit yourself to the circumstances of today, you can pray eagerly and openhandedly for a husband if that is your good desire. Ask other saints to join you in praying. Don't hold back in your asking. You can rest assured He will do what's best and you must do what children do—ask your Father for what you want, according to His will.

LOVE'S BANNER FLIES OVER YOU

My friend survived the difficult days surrounding the ending of her engagement. She didn't just survive them, she began to blossom through them. There was more lightness in her step, more laughter in her eyes, more freedom in her voice. Why? Because in ending that engagement, she had by no means left her chance for love behind. Instead, the One who loved her best, loved her still. Her Savior who beckoned her away from the sorrows of being married to an unbeliever whose selfishness had led him to hurt her physically, was not beckoning her away from love but toward it. Of course, Jesus is not a personal boyfriend. He's not someone who takes the place of personal romantic love in an earthly sense. But He is the source of love—the lover of our souls whose love never fails. And the church, made up of all His people, is His bride. He is our bridegroom.

At the end of the age, when Christ returns to judge the living and the dead, He will do what King Solomon did with His actual bride: He will bring His people—His bride—into the banquet room to feast and His banner over us will be love. He calls this the marriage supper of the Lamb, and every one of us, whether we were married in this life or single, will be a part of it, for we will finally and fully be united to Him forever. No more longing, no more sorrow, no more sin. We, the church, will feast on Mount Zion with our Savior, our Friend, our King, our Groom, our God.

Main Point

Singleness and marriage can both be lived out in ways that are honoring to the Lord.

Questions for Reflection

- What has God called you to today—marriage or singleness? How can you glorify Him today in that calling?
- If you desire to be married someday, have you considered praying and asking God for a godly husband? Who could join you in praying for this?
- How can you cultivate contentment even as you ask God for something big that He hasn't yet given you?

9. Owning Our Agency

So when the woman saw that the tree was good for food, and that it was a delight to the eyes, and that the tree was to be desired to make one wise, she took of its fruit and ate, and she also gave some to her husband who was with her, and he ate. (Gen. 3:6)

When I went off to college, I suppose you could say I was naïve. At least, that's what one professor kept telling me and the rest of the students. He seemed to relish informing us that our faith, which couldn't possibly be real given our age and naivety, would soon be relinquished and exchanged for something less certain, a different sort of faith that would see the value in exploring and embracing doubt and ambiguity, a faith that could let go of the beliefs of our parents and distinguish itself. This, we were to understand, was a laudable goal.

But, as an earnest and hopeful eighteen-year-old, I didn't really see how embracing doubt or abandoning the faith of my parents fit with following God or honoring my parents, things I knew for sure God wanted me to do (because He'd actually told me so in His book!). I guess my naivety was in believing that an older Christian, like my professor, thought that the truth of the Bible was, well, actually true, and that the goodness of the Good News was, well, really good.

That wasn't the only surprising thing I'd hear from a college professor. Another one wanted to make sure we knew what a trial it was to be a woman. She wanted us to understand the injustice of simply having been born a woman. This was new information for me. What I mean is, I certainly knew women (some very close to me) who had experienced great trials and been victims in one sense or another of a person's sin, but to orient the entire category of womanhood around victimhood was not something I'd seen done.

My experience revealed that not all women had the same experiences of suffering or being sinned against. I knew I wasn't a victim—I knew that whatever minor injustices I'd experienced from others were paltry when I contemplated my own assault on God's holiness. And it seemed to me that turning womanhood into victimhood writ large mocked the legacy of countless women who endured terrible difficulties, yet still never related to the world as victims. Claiming such a status for myself would not only have been dishonest, but disrespectful.

POWERLESS VICTIMS OR ABLE TO ACT?

When Satan enters the garden as told in Genesis 3, he approaches Eve and begins speaking to her. We know that he effectively deceives her into believing that if she were to eat the fruit from the tree of the knowledge of good and evil, that—rather than die as God had told Adam would happen—she would be like God. Later, when Paul is explaining why women may not teach or have authority over men in the church, he gives two reasons. First, because the man was formed first then the woman (order of creation), and second, because the woman was deceived and became a transgressor. (1 Tim. 2:13-14)

In other words, being lied to and deceived did not make Eve a victim. Why not? Because she still had a choice to make, even though the serpent's lie was evil. It is still a sin to believe a lie, especially when God has told you the truth. Believing God is the foundation of faith and evidence that you're His child. There are many in this world who want you to believe that your biggest problem in life is what happens to you—that your life circumstances (or others' circumstances) are the main obstacles to all being well in the world. Therefore, working to change those circumstances in life and society becomes a sort of works-based salvation.

But the picture the Bible paints of us is that the sin inside us is our biggest problem. Other people's sin against us can harm us, but other people's sin does not cause us to sin nor absolve us of a sinful response. Our sin makes us God's enemies; we have a heart of stone and a rebellious spirit toward Him. Eve didn't merely need God to rescue her from being Satan's victim (although Satan certainly did manipulate her). She needed God to rescue her from the sin and death that now reigned in her whole self because she chose to believe a lie from a serpent rather than the very words of the Lord. And the Lord's words proved true— death did come for Adam and Eve. The curse of sin is real and we feel its effects keenly, even today.

But, the good news is that, because of the powerful grace of God at work in us because of Christ, once we've been born again, we are able not to sin! 'For sin will have no dominion over you, since you are not under law but under grace.' (Rom. 6:14) Not only has God given us a pardon by His Son's blood, He has given us power by His Spirit to turn from sin. We have *agency*. And in the new heavens and new earth, when we're finally glorified and our sanctification is complete, we will be unable to sin.

AN ADDICTING CURRENCY THAT KILLS

I never accepted the idea my professor tried to instill in us that womanhood is victimhood. After searching the Scriptures, I realized that to accept womanhood as victimhood would mean believing that the injustices committed by men and women against each other weighed heavier in the scales than our own sin against a holy God. Also, while God cares very much about the injustice that happens horizontally between humans, He never sees people in one-dimensional ways. He can see the injustice done to us *and* the sin in our own hearts and actions. He can act for justice on behalf of one who is in need of it, while simultaneously holding that same one responsible for their sin.

And then there's Jesus.

Jesus, who lived perfectly, yet was sinned against over and over. Jesus, who committed no injustice, yet bore the injustices of world. Was He a victim? Jesus says that no one took His life from Him, but that He laid it down of His own accord. (John 10:18) Furthermore, Isaiah tells us that it was the will of God to crush His Son. This doesn't negate the fact that the men who put Jesus to death were sinning against Him. He was, in an earthly sense, a victim of their sinfulness. But we know that this was not the complete story. He was not a victim, but rather the Victor who reigned even as He hung on the cross! The plans of sinful men were wielded in the hand of a loving Father. So too, for all God's children.

Yet the mentality of victimhood is still alluring to many women. It still persuades women to think about themselves as lacking agency, lacking the ability to act in a meaningful way, and primarily subject to the actions of others. It's persuasive because there is enough truth in it to turn our heads. Sometimes we do lack agency. Sometimes other people have forcibly abused or harmed us. Sometimes our circumstances seem more difficult than we can bear. Our youngest son has disabilities and the two hardest things about it are: 1) that he didn't sleep well for years and years, and 2) his seizures are life-threatening and have landed him on life support twice. You can imagine that these realities have garnered a fair amount of sympathy for him and our family. But sometimes, I wanted even more than sympathy and prayers and support from others—I was tempted to form an identity of victimhood because of the trials of disability. I was tempted to use it as an excuse for bad behavior and a never-ending supply of non-judgmental attention.

Victimhood, in this culture, buys you status. It earns you constant sympathy that does not ask for anything in return. Most importantly, it makes you unassailable, unable to be tried in the court of public morality, free from accountability. And if you think women are the only ones who've figured this little trick out, just look at the multiplying victim identities and observe how men have found their way into them. Women may have gotten there first, but now their claim to ultimate victimhood has backfired, as men who identify as women have trumped their previously unattainable victim card.

Claiming victimhood *as an identity* misunderstands the characters in the story God has written. As we already saw, Eve wasn't a victim in the garden, she was the one perpetrating the crime. She stole God's fruit. She disobeyed God's instructions. And Adam, who absolutely knew better, did the same. Were they the villains in the story? No, the villain was the serpent. But they did what they did. And God held them accountable for it. To turn womanhood into victimhood is to mis-remember the story. But, even more, it keeps us from rightly understanding the rest of the story. It keeps us from repentance and faith, because it keeps us thinking we didn't do anything wrong. It keeps us believing that we deserve so much better than what we're getting, rather than seeing that we are awash in God's kindness in holding back His wrath for sin and patiently waiting for His people to turn to Him in repentance.

Victimhood, as an identity, ultimately finds fault with God, who is sovereign over our suffering and our circumstances. It cannot stomach Romans 8:28, 'that for those who love God all things work together for good, for those who are called according to his purpose.'

So how should you respond when you see 'MeToo' hashtags popping up over social media, or 'Time's Up' protests near your school? With compassion, readiness to listen, and an acknowledgement that sexism and violence against women are all too real. The disunity between the sexes is a tragic reality that has been present in minor and major ways since the fall. Maybe you've experienced a taste of this injustice yourself. It's important to treat abuse seriously, and to confide in someone you trust if you or someone you know has been abused.

But of all the identities the world wants you to adopt, I beg you, run from the mentality of victimhood and to the powerful arms of your Savior. What you'll discover is that God has given more power to women than most of us could dream if we'd simply be willing to see it. It's not the sort of power that flashes thunder bolts or wins big awards or impresses the world, but it is eternally potent nonetheless. It is the power of His Holy Spirit that quietly shapes and influences everything around it for good.

Dear sisters, with the Holy Spirit of the all-powerful living God at work in you, can you ever rightly think of yourself as a victim? With God working all things, even your trials and the sins of others against you, for your good, can you rightly indulge in self-pity? Rather, the Spirit at work in you is one of power and love and self-control. It is one of love and joy and peace. All of us—women who are in Christ—can rightly say with Paul:

Who shall separate us from the love of Christ? Shall tribulation, or distress, or persecution, or famine, or nakedness, or danger, or sword? As it is written,

'For your sake we are being killed all the day long;
     we are regarded as sheep to be slaughtered.'

No, in all these things we are more than conquerors through him who loved us. (Rom. 8:35-37)

'More than conquerors through him who loved us.' That's who we are, even in tribulation. Don't ever, ever forget it.

Main Point

Though you may have been hurt, don't make the mistake of finding identity in victimhood.

Questions for Reflection

- Have you ever observed 'victim mentality'? What are some of the hallmarks of it?
- Can you think of a time when you were tempted toward that mentality? How did you withstand the temptation?
- How can you keep a soft heart and willing hands to help people who have been truly sinned against or victimized in a given situation, while also steering clear of the mindset that lays blame at God's feet for the injustice in the world?

10. What Will Being a Christian Woman Cost Me?

Then they will deliver you up to tribulation and put you to death, and you will be hated by all nations for my name's sake. And then many will fall away and betray one another and hate one another. And many false prophets will arise and lead many astray. And because lawlessness will be increased, the love of many will grow cold. But the one who endures to the end will be saved. And this gospel of the kingdom will be proclaimed throughout the whole world as a testimony to all nations, and then the end will come. (Matt. 24:9-14)

'With every eye closed and every head bowed, I want you to raise your hand if you accept Jesus into your heart. No one is looking. This is just between you and the Lord.'

It was a speech I heard many times growing up. The pastor who gave it had a heart that longed for people to know Jesus. He was doing all he could to lead people to the Living Water. But there is something very different in the call to follow Jesus he gave, and the stark warning Jesus had for His disciples when He said, '... you will be hated by all nations for my name's sake.' (Matt. 24:9) Jesus' words were a sort of anti-altar call. He ensures there will be no easy believe-ism happening. Instead, He tells His band of followers that to pledge allegiance to Jesus means you will lose everything else. His followers would be hated, betrayed, persecuted, and killed.

Perhaps twenty years ago, the idea of being delivered up to die for your allegiance to Christ and His Word was quaint and far-off. But over the last several years, it has appeared less so. I do not know anyone in the United States who has been physically harmed or put to death for being a Christian, but I do know people who've lost their jobs and their ability to provide for their family. I've seen people canceled online for their Christian beliefs, with threats of violence and reputations hurt because of slander. And, although very small in scale, I have experienced the hatred and reviling of those who can't abide the Word of God incarnate, Jesus, and are particularly angry when they hear His words in my mouth.

What's perhaps surprising is how much the disdain of one's peers can silence professed Christians. Without any threat of violence, disdain and disapproval are a powerful tool to keep this generation quiet when it comes to speaking the truth of God's Word.

TRUSTING THE PARACHUTE ENOUGH TO JUMP

It always comes back to what we really believe. By 'believe,' I don't mean what you assent to intellectually and theoretically. I may say, 'I believe that parachutes are safe to use when jumping from an airplane.' But who would think I was telling the truth if, in my moment of need, I then refused to jump from an airplane with one? The statement may have been truthful in a sort of disconnected intellectual way—I really may think they are safe. But the belief must be tested out in real life to show itself to be faith.

We may have all sorts of intellectual beliefs about God, what it means to be women, and how His gospel transforms us. They may be genuinely-held beliefs. Most of us don't try to be hypocrites; we just haven't ever been put in a situation where the parachute we said was safe was put on our own back and we had to rely on the fabric holding fast amid the rushing wind of descent.

Living at the time we live in right now means that trying to convince someone to become a Christian because it will make their life easier or because it's really fun or because you'll have lots of amazing and popular friends, is just stupid and untrue. To be fair, it's always been stupid to try to get people to Jesus that way. But it hasn't always been untrue, until more recently. The fringe benefits of allegiance to Christ in the USA are evaporating. We live in a world where, increasingly, Jesus' hard sell makes more sense.

There is no way around it. Jesus demands everything. 'And he said to all, "If anyone would come after me, let him deny himself and take up his cross daily and follow me."' (Luke 9:23) He also says,

Whoever loves father or mother more than me is not worthy of me, and whoever loves son or daughter more than me is not worthy of me. And whoever does not take his cross and follow me is not worthy of me. Whoever

finds his life will lose it, and whoever loses his life for my sake will find it. (Matt. 10:37-39)

When Jesus tells us that He is the way, the truth, and the life, I think too many want the truth with the edges sanded down a bit more. But Jesus is bold and direct with the truth because He actually loves us. He doesn't patronize us, He doesn't distort love into lying or flattery so as not to offend; instead, He tells us the truth that will cost us everything in order that we might find life in Him.

So, should you go sell all you have this moment? Write your parents out of your will? Rethink having children since they might tempt you to love them more than Jesus? No, no, and no. Rather, you must die—every bit of you and all your worldly loyalties along with you. Die to every allegiance you ever had, especially the allegiance you have to yourself. Then, when God raises you from the dead with new life in His Son, watch how nothing is the same. When He raises you from the dead, you will love your parents, but not in a self-serving way. You will love them for God's sake. When He raises you from the dead, you will likely have possessions, but you will no longer possess them as you did before, rather you will steward them for God's sake.

GENDER: AN ISSUE YOU CAN'T IGNORE

Different time periods have had different flash points that show us what mattered to the people who lived then. One primary way the world we live in now has moved away from Christ is to reject His supremacy over creation—namely, male and female. Colossians says:

> He is the image of the invisible God, the firstborn of all creation. For by him all things were created, in heaven and on earth, visible and invisible, whether thrones or dominions or rulers or authorities—all things were created through him and for him. And he is before all things, and in him all things hold together. And he is the head of the body, the church. He is the beginning, the firstborn from the dead, that in everything he might be preeminent. (Col. 1:15-18)

All things were made through and for Christ—including male and female. If you want to know the issue that will cost you friendships and strain family relations and keep you from getting the job you want and make you a stench to your neighbors, this is it. This is where the culture has drawn a line and said, *You must agree with us on this.* If you don't, there will be a high price—from corporate policies that make it impossible for a Bible-believing Christian to maintain employment, to a public school curriculum that abuses young minds, to hate speech laws that protect sexual deviance and idolatry as sacred—none of us can hide from the gender reckoning.

This is where we may be prone to soft-pedal, when what we need to do is remember Jesus' hard sell. When we see the world making gender the defining moral issue (or rather immoral issue) of the day, we may think it a good time for some introspection about how hard it must be to be gay or trans or any of the other gender identities. And if we make that our primary focus, we've already lost the battle. Of course it's hard to be LGBTQ. It's hard because sin is a cruel master. The solution is not to get inside the perspective of sin and the hatred of God's ways and start sympathizing with it. The solution is to remember how Jesus loved us by telling us the truth—the hard sell. What our LGBTQ-supporting friends and neighbors need to know is that God demands everything of them, just like He does of us. Including their sin-sick ideas about gender and sexuality. He requires *all*, because to require less would be to leave us in our sin.

LGBTQ-identifying people and their advocates are worshiping an idol when it comes to gender. The idol's name is Self-Creator, but the Self-Creator has a problem—it can't make anything. It can only distort things that have already been made. We have a better word to speak to them. The better word is Christ— Christ, who made them male or female; Christ, who can redeem them; Christ, who gives them a purpose: they were made *for* Him.

Your life, as a woman who embraces being made a woman, helps to speak this better word. Your steadfast acceptance and reception of the gift of womanhood is a testimony in our broken culture. Your being unashamed of the gospel of Jesus Christ and unashamed to be called His *daughter,* is a witness to the world that God is good and He does good. Your love for all of God's words and ways in the Bible, including the words that apply directly to women—and your obedience to them—are a powerful means to stopping the mouths of revilers, as Titus 2:5 says. Do not forsake your ordinary life as a holy woman of God. Live it as a testimony of His grace.

THE 10,000 YEAR COST-BENEFIT ANALYSIS

We can feel pretty lightweight when the stiff winds of cultural change seem to be against us. It's not easy for us mere mortals to swim against the current when the current is strong. But, there is a deeper current, a current of sovereign purpose and love that will very soon overcome all the small streams that would try to challenge it. When we believe ourselves to be standing alone against the tide, we must let the Lord remind us, 'What then shall we say to these things? If God is for us, who can be against us? He who did not spare his own Son but gave him up for us all, how will he not also with him graciously give us all things?' (Rom. 8:31-32).

When God is for us, those who are against us account to nothing when all is said and done. When we have lost our friends or family or jobs or status for the sake of Christ, we have gained Him, and with Him *all things*. Paul put it this way, 'For I consider that the sufferings of this present time are not worth comparing with the glory that is to be revealed to us' (Rom. 8:18).

Whatever the cost now, it doesn't compare to the eternal benefit.

But there are joys to be counted now, too, not just in the age to come. Did you know there is great joy in calling sin sin and calling God's holiness holy? That when we see sin for what it is and reject it, we are living in true freedom? Did you know there is great gladness in agreeing with God about every last thing— in letting Him be God and Author (the one with the *authority*) and you be His child? And did you know there is an immeasurable hope and joy that comes in the fellowship of suffering with Christ? The hope that is produced in our suffering is the hope of the resurrection and *that hope does not put us to shame.* (Rom. 5:5)

Someday, in the near or far-off future, when following Jesus starts to cost you more than you think you can bear, you may wonder if it's worth it to trust Christ. You may wonder if it's worth it to live as a *Christian woman* in the midst of such difficulty and darkness. It's in that moment when Christ will be everything, for He will be the light to guide you, the water to fill you, the bread to sustain you, the shepherd to comfort you, and the door to bring you into His presence. Even the darkness is as light to

Him. (Ps. 129:12) There is no loss that isn't gain in Christ.

In 10,000 years, I would have you happy and whole, daughters of the Living God. Let's live like it now with the eager expectation of glory to come.

Main Point

Debates around womanhood and sexuality have become the battlelines for faithful Christianity in our culture. Live as a testimony to God's truth.

Questions for Reflection

- Do you agree that sexuality is the primary issue today where Christians will face persecution and rejection from the world? Why or why not?
- Have you considered Jesus' 'hard sell' approach to making disciples? How is this different or similar to what you've heard in church?
- Have you counted the cost of being an unashamed Christian woman? What might it cost you personally? Have you counted the joys of being an unashamed Christian woman?

Appendix A: What Now?

- Try to identify areas in your thinking about sex and gender that have been influenced by the world and are out of step with God's Word.
- Spend time in the Scriptures meditating on the goodness of God's plan in making male and female in His image, yet profoundly unique in their bodies and roles.
- Praise God for making you a woman. Ask Him to deepen your gladness in being what He made you.
- Consider how being a Christian and living in submission to God helps give shape and meaning to your womanhood.
- How can you cultivate habits that keep you attuned to hearing God's voice in His Word over and above all the voices in the world?
- Ask your pastor or a godly friend if they have a Bible reading plan they recommend.

- What godly women can you look to for support, encouragement, and instruction as you seek to grow as a virtuous woman who fears the Lord?
- Remember that God is sovereign over every situation in your life, including singleness and marriage. Trust that He is working for your good in all things.
- How might you seek to influence the younger women around you in a way that honors God and His design? How can you help them give thanks for being made a woman by God?
- Prepare yourself to be disliked and mistreated for agreeing with God (and disagreeing with the world) about what it means to be male and female. Rejoice and be glad in that day!

Appendix B: Other Books and Resources

STARTING OUT

Elisabeth Elliot, *Let Me Be A Woman* (Wheaton, IL: Tyndale House, 1999)

Abigail Dodds, *(A)Typical Woman: Free, Whole, and Called in Christ* (Wheaton, IL: Crossway, 2019)

Rebekah Merkle, *Eve in Exile and the Restoration of Femininity* (Moscow, ID: Canon Press, 2016)

DIGGING DEEPER

Kevin DeYoung, *Men and Women in the Church: A Short, Biblical, Practical Introduction* (Wheaton, IL: Crossway, 2021)

Margaret E. Köstenberger, *Jesus and the Feminists: Who Do They Say That He Is?* (Wheaton, IL: Crossway, 2008)

MORE PLEASE!

Herman Bavinck, *The Christian Family* (Grand Rapids, MI: Christian's Library Press, 2012)

Alexander Strauch, *Equal Yet Different: A Brief Study on the Biblical Passages on Gender* (Colorado Springs, CO: Lewis & Roth Publishers, 1999)

Watch out for other forthcoming books in the
Track series, including:

Gaming (2022)
Justification (2022)
Depression (2022)
Worldview (2022)
Missions (2022)
Prayer
Body Image
Dating & Marriage
Music
Social Media
Apologetics

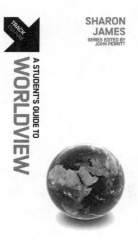

SHARON
JAMES
SERIES EDITED BY
JOHN PERRITT

A STUDENT'S GUIDE TO
WORLDVIEW

A Student's Guide to
Worldview

Sharon James

We all view the world through a certain lens.
Depending on our upbringing, geography,
experiences and a whole host of other influences,
we will see life a certain way. Our understanding
of truth, justice, love, and good and evil is shaped
by what we hear and are taught. Using real–life
stories and poignant historical overviews, Sharon
James writes to equip the next generation with the
wisdom needed to think through some of the most
divisive cultural issues of our day.

978-1-5271-0843-1

A Student's Guide to Missions

Emilio Garofalo Neto

All of us have someone else to thank for receiving the good news of salvation. Mission is a means to a greater goal – God's name being glorified in the salvation of sinners. We should long to see God's fame being spread as far as possible. Throughout the Bible God chose to reach the nations through the preaching of His own people. Emilio Garofalo Neto helps us think through mission, the place it has in our world today, and our role in the mission of Christ.

978-1-5271-0896-7

A Student's Guide to the Power of Story

Joe Deegan

Stories are powerful. They shape us and stay with us in a way that nothing else does. Ideas and wisdom can be portrayed in a way that draws the listener or reader in. Stories can build relationships and understanding. They can help to make sense of confusing concepts. In this compelling addition to the *Track* series, Joe Deegan explains why stories are so important – and what role they play in our everyday lives.

978-1-5271-0695-6

A Student's Guide to
Navigating Culture

WALT MUELLER

We all belong to a culture. From the shows we watch to the language we use to the food we eat; culture shapes the way we look at the world, the way we act, the way we think. It affects so much of our lives, and yet we are rarely aware of it. If we are not careful, it can push us away from God's good desires for who we are and how we live in our world.

978-1-5271-0694-9

LIGON DUNCAN
& JOHN PERRITT

A STUDENT'S GUIDE TO
SANCTIFICATION

A Student's Guide to Sanctification

LIGON DUNCAN & JOHN PERRITT

Knowing that we have been saved by what Jesus has done rather than by what we have done is amazing. But how does this knowledge affect the way we live? What's the point in being good if we will be forgiven anyway? Actually the Bible says that God's forgiveness frees us to live for Him and through the Holy Spirit we can grow to become more and more like Jesus. Ligon Duncan and John Perritt dive into what that means in this short book.

978-1-5271-0451-8

EDWARD T.
WELCH

A Student's Guide to Anxiety

Edward T. Welch

We all know the feeling. That nervous, jittery, tense feeling that tells you that something bad is just ahead. Anxiety can be overwhelming. But the Bible has plenty to say to people who are anxious. This book will help us to take our eyes off our circumstances and fix them on God.

978-1-5271-0450-1

Reformed Youth Ministries (RYM) exists to serve the Church in reaching and equipping youth for Christ. Passing on the faith to the next generation has been RYM's mission since it began. In 1972, three youth workers who shared a passion for biblical teaching to high school students surveyed the landscape of youth ministry conferences. What they found was a primary emphasis on fun and games, not God's Word. They launched a conference that focused on the preaching and teaching of God's Word – RYM. Over the last five decades RYM has grown from a single summer conference into three areas of ministry: conferences, training, and resources.

- **Conferences:** RYM hosts multiple summer conferences for local church groups in a variety of locations across the United States. Conferences are for either middle school or high school students and their leaders.
- **Training:** RYM launched an annual Youth Leader Training (YLT) event in 2008. YLT is

for anyone serving with youth in the local church. YLT has grown steadily through the years and is now offered in multiple locations. RYM also offers a Church Internship Program in partnering local churches, youth leader coaching and youth ministry consulting services.

- **Resources:** RYM offers a growing array of resources for leaders, parents, and students. Several BIble studies are available as free downloads (new titles regularly added). RYM hosts multiple podcasts available on numerous platforms: The Local Youth Worker, Parenting Today, and The RYM Student Podcast. To access free downloads, for podcast information, and access to many additional ministry tools visit us on the web – rym.org.

RYM is a 501(c)(3) non-profit organization. Our mission is made possible through the generous support of individuals, churches, foundations and businesses that share our mission to serve the Church in reaching and equipping youth for Christ. If you would like to partner with RYM in reaching and equipping the next generation for Christ please visit rym.org/donate.

Christian Focus Publications

Our mission statement —

STAYING FAITHFUL

In dependence upon God we seek to impact the world through literature faithful to His infallible Word, the Bible. Our aim is to ensure that the Lord Jesus Christ is presented as the only hope to obtain forgiveness of sin, live a useful life and look forward to heaven with Him.

Our books are published in four imprints:

CHRISTIAN
FOCUS

Popular works including biographies, commentaries, basic doctrine and Christian living.

CHRISTIAN
HERITAGE

Books representing some of the best material from the rich heritage of the church.

MENTOR

Books written at a level suitable for Bible College and seminary students, pastors, and other serious readers. The imprint includes commentaries, doctrinal studies, examination of current issues and church history.

CF4•K

Children's books for quality Bible teaching and for all age groups: Sunday school curriculum, puzzle and activity books; personal and family devotional titles, biographies and inspirational stories — because you are never too young to know Jesus!

Christian Focus Publications Ltd,
Geanies House, Fearn, Ross-shire,
IV20 1TW, Scotland, United Kingdom.
www.christianfocus.com
blog.christianfocus.com

Today, many claim that the Bible is bad news for women. Nothing could be further from the truth! In this accessible and engaging book, Abigail Dodds shows that God's creation design is good news—for all of us!

Sharon James
Author of several books, including *God's Design for Women in an Age of Gender Confusion* and *Gender Ideology: What do Christians need to Know?*

Do you know that there is eternal purpose and meaning to your womanhood? It runs deeper than your skin, your clothes, your relationships, and even your self-perception. With honesty, wisdom, and clarity, Abigail Dodds reveals that God's vision for our gender, our bodies, our singleness, our marriage, is so much bigger than that of the world. And Abigail strengthens our arms: demonstrating that though we live in a battle to preserve God's biblical womanhood, we are not victims but women victorious in Christ!

Natalie Brand
Author of several books, including *Prone to Wander: Grace for the Lukewarm and Apathetic,* and *The Good Portion – Salvation: The Doctrine of Salvation, for Every Woman*

Womanhood is God's good gift to humanity, and this book is a gift to the church. Crucial for today's cultural climate when our kids are being conformed to the world's ideas of identity, *Track: Womanhood* compellingly calls girls and young women to rejoice in who they truly are. Moms, discuss this book with your daughters! Youth group leaders, pass these out generously! Pre-teen and teenage girls, read *Track: Womanhood* and think deeply about what it means for you to be a woman.

Keri Folmar
Pastor's wife,
the Evangelical Christian Church of Dubai
Author of *The Good Portion: Scripture*, as well as
How Can Women Thrive in the Local Church and the
Delighting in the Word Bible Study Series